HISTORY'S SECRET GROUPS

AC Cashiers Comm. Library
P.O. Box 2127
Cashiers NC 28717

by Tammy Gagne

www.12StoryLibrary.com

Copyright © 2019 by 12-Story Library, Mankato, MN 56003. All rights reserved. No part of this book may be reproduced or utilized in any form or by any means without written permission from the publisher.

12-Story Library is an imprint of Bookstaves.

Photographs © CC0, cover, 1; PD, 4; Nevit Dilmen/CC3.0, 5; Archivist/Alamy Stock Photo, 6; François Séraphin Delpech/PD, 7; Eluveitie/CC3.0, 8; In-Finity/Shutterstock.com, 8; Library of Congress, 9; Sam Hood/PD, 10; Sheridan Libraries/Levy/Gado/Getty Images, 11; PD, 12; Classic Image/Alamy Stock Photo, 13; CC4.0, 14; PD, 15; Everett Historical/Shutterstock.com, 16; Library of Congress, 17; Marion Dunlap Harper/CC3.0, 18; Robert Thall/Library of Congress, 19; PD, 20; PD, 21; Bettmann/Getty Images, 22; PD, 23; Michiel1972/CC4.0, 24; Hi-Point/Shutterstock.com, 25; PD, 26; CC0, 27; Everett Historical/Shutterstock.com, 28; PD, 29

ISBN
978-1-63235-597-3 (hardcover)
978-1-63235-651-2 (paperback)
978-1-63235-710-6 (ebook)

Library of Congress Control Number: 2018947733

Printed in the United States of America
Mankato, MN
July 2018

About the Cover
Members of the notorious Black Hand Society around 1910. Its leader, Dragutin Dimitrijević, is standing back right.

Access free, up-to-date content on this topic plus a full digital version of this book. Scan the QR code on page 31 or use your school's login at 12StoryLibrary.com.

Table of Contents

Skull and Bones: Not Just a College Club 4

Knights Templar: Warriors of the Crusades 6

Freemasons: Secrecy and Charity 8

Odd Fellows: International Do-Gooders 10

Illuminati: Secrecy and Mystery 12

Hashashin: Fearsome Assassins 14

Molly Maguires: Fighting for Workers' Rights 16

P.E.O. Sisterhood: Women Helping Women 18

Golden Dawn Society: Magic and the Occult 20

IBPOE: Elks for Blacks 22

Bilderberg Group: Global Secrecy 24

Black Hand Society: The Spark That Started WWI 26

Fact Sheet 28

Glossary 30

For More Information 31

Index 32

About the Author 32

Skull and Bones: Not Just a College Club

Members of the Order of the Skull and Bones have included three US presidents. More than 20 US senators have belonged. So have dozens of well-known business leader. Members are called Bonesmen.

Skull and Bones was formed at Yale University in 1832 as a social club. One of its founders was Alphonso Taft, future father to US President William Howard Taft. Only Yale students can be Bonesmen. And they can't just decide to join. They have to be invited. Most members have been white men from rich and powerful families. They must swear complete allegiance to the club.

Many conspiracy theories have sprung up about Skull and Bones. Some people believe members take part in crimes or other shady activities. Some even think Bonesmen were behind the assassination of US President John F. Kennedy in 1963.

The Skull and Bones headquarters in Connecticut.

Over time, Skull and Bones has changed. Women are now allowed to be members. So are people of different races. Family wealth and influence are no longer the most important qualifications. But the order is still very secretive. Its headquarters in New Haven, Connecticut, is a windowless building called the Tomb. Skull and Bones owns a private island near the university where only members can go.

15
Number of Yale students invited to join Skull and Bones each year.

- Skull and Bones was established in 1832 as a social club.
- Many rich and powerful people have been part of the group.
- Skull and Bones has changed, but it's still very secretive.

A SHORT LIST OF SKULL AND BONES MEMBERS

Members of Skull and Bones have included US presidents William Howard Taft, George H.W. Bush, and George W. Bush. US Supreme Court Justice Potter Stewart was a member. So was former US senator, secretary of state, and presidential candidate John Kerry. And Steven Mnuchin, US treasury secretary under President Donald Trump.

Knights Templar: Warriors of the Crusades

The Knights Templar was a large Christian society in Europe during the Crusades. Its purpose was to protect pilgrims who were visiting holy sites. Travelers to the sites were often robbed and even killed.

A French knight named Hugues de Payens started the society around 1118. At first, it was called the Poor Knights of Christ and the Temple of Solomon. Members were deeply religious. Many were skilled military men. They weren't allowed to gamble, swear, or drink alcohol. They couldn't own property or get married. Their main duty was to fight.

Over time, the Knights Templar became very powerful. Governments and other organizations across Europe supported the society. It acquired large pieces of land and built great wealth. Some people felt the society was too powerful. In 1307, King Philip IV of France had many members arrested and killed. He took away the group's riches. By 1312, the Knights Templar had been dissolved.

A 12th-century Knights Templar member providing protection.

SPECIAL RIGHTS

In 1139, Pope Innocent II gave special rights to the Knights Templar. Members didn't have to pay taxes. They could build their own chapels. And the only laws they had to follow were the pope's. Some people didn't like that the Knights Templar received this special treatment. They said the pope's action showed the group had too much power.

20,000
Approximate number of members in Knights Templar at group's peak.

- The Knights Templar protected Christian pilgrims traveling to holy sites.
- Its members were skilled military men with strong religious beliefs.
- After gaining great wealth and influence, the society was dissolved.

When Philip IV died suddenly in 1314 at age 42, some said that was God's revenge.

Some people think the group still exists in secret. There are many conspiracy theories about it. Writers have spun stories about the Knights Templar.

King Philip IV of France.

3

Freemasons: Secrecy and Charity

The Freemasons are one of the world's largest secret societies. The group's roots go back to at least 1600. Medieval stoneworkers, or masons, started the society.

Over time, the Freemasons became a social group. The society also performed charity work. In 1717, the first grand lodge opened in London. By this point, most members were not stoneworkers. They accepted members from many different backgrounds. This made them controversial.

The Freemasons are still controversial. Many nonmembers are suspicious of them. That's because the society has always been secretive. Information on group activities is never shared publicly. Meetings and rituals take place behind closed lodge doors.

Some people think the Freemasons are doing illegal things. Others don't go this far. But they do claim the group hides its influence. Rumors say Freemasons control the government. It's believed that society members steer world economies to make themselves rich.

The grand lodge in London.

US President George Washington depicted as a Freemason.

But there's no proof to rumors like these.

It's true that many Freemasons have been powerful men. US presidents George Washington, Franklin D. Roosevelt, and Gerald Ford were members. Other famous Freemasons include magician Harry Houdini and actor John Wayne.

THE SHRINERS

The Freemasons have many subgroups. One of the biggest is the Shriners. Like other Freemasons, Shriners are dedicated to charity work. Their focus is health care. The organization has 22 hospitals across the United States. Patients at these hospitals don't have to pay for medical services.

6 million
Estimated number of Freemasons worldwide.

- Freemasonry has its roots in Europe.
- Many people are suspicious of Freemasons because members are secretive.
- Freemasons include many powerful and famous people.

Odd Fellows: International Do-Gooders

The Independent Order of Odd Fellows was formed in England during the early 1700s. By the 1800s, groups had sprung up in other countries around the world.

The society was established by English laborers. Its purpose was to help other everyday people who were going through hard times. Life was not easy for many people in the 1700s. They worked hard, often for little pay. Disease was common. And people who got sick often died. Many families struggled to pay medical bills and burial costs for loved ones. The Odd Fellows banded together to help each other.

In 1819, the Odd Fellows came to the United States. The first US lodge opened in Baltimore, Maryland. At the time, there was a yellow fever epidemic in the city. Odd Fellows visited people who were sick. They helped families bury their dead.

And they took responsibility for educating children who were orphaned.

For many years, only men could join the Odd Fellows. But in 1851, the society became the first US fraternity to accept women. The women are not called Odd Fellows. They are called Daughters of Rebekah.

Odd Fellows and Rebekahs exist to do charitable acts. But some outsiders don't trust them. Rumors have suggested the Odd Fellows are up to illegal things. None of the rumors have been proven true.

Cover of sheet music composed for a Rebekahs' march.

26
Number of countries with Odd Fellows lodges.

- The Odd Fellows was established in England during the 1700s.
- Odd Fellows lodges around the world give money and support to people in need.
- Some people are suspicious of the Odd Fellows and spread rumors about the society.

THINK ABOUT IT

Think of a time when you did something kind for another person. How did that make you feel? Why do you think some people are suspicious of people who do charitable acts?

5 Illuminati: Secrecy and Mystery

The Illuminati is a very mysterious secret society. It was founded on May 1, 1776, by a German university professor named Adam Weishaupt. He and four other men met in a forest. Lit by flickering torches, they set the rules for their group. New people could join only if all the other members approved. People chosen for the Illuminati had to have good reputations. They had to be from wealthy families and have useful social connections.

The Illuminati felt that kings and the Church were limiting freedom of thought. Their goal was to create a state of liberty and equality. Early members were Weishaupt's students. Over time, the group welcomed politicians, doctors, lawyers, and other professionals. Many well-known and successful people were said to be members. One was the powerful banker Mayer Amschel Rothschild. Another was the famous writer Johann Wolfgang von Goethe. Today people around the world claim to be Illuminati. The internet is full of rumors.

More conspiracy theories have swirled around the Illuminati than

13
Number of Degrees, or status levels, an Illuminati member can reach.

- German professor Adam Weishaupt founded the Illuminati during the 1700s.
- Members were respected people with wealth and power.
- Some people say the society wants to rule the world.

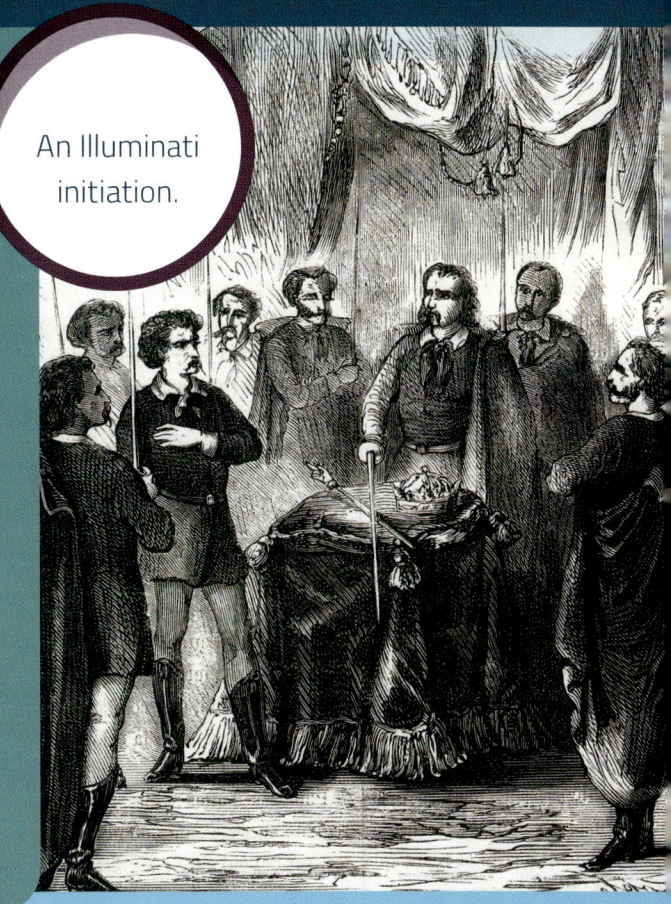

An Illuminati initiation.

THE END OF THE REAL ILLUMINATI

The Illuminati founded by Adam Weishaupt had a short life. In 1785, the leader of Bavaria issued an order banning the Illuminati. Its members were arrested. Another order in 1787 imposed the death penalty for membership. Weishaupt was banished. The real Illuminati were officially over … but the legend lives on.

almost any other secret group. It's been said they were behind the French Revolution. That they want to divide and rule the world. The Illuminati have become part of pop culture. Some characters in best-selling novels, comic books, and movies are described as Illuminati.

Hashashin: Fearsome Assassins

The Hashashin were one of the most feared secret societies of all time. The word assassin comes from their name. Little is known about this Islamic sect, except they killed people.

It's said the Hashashin were led by a secretive Old Man of the Mountain. He is often called Shaykh-al-Hashishim. He lived in the mountains of Iran and Syria during the 1100s. He educated men and trained them to kill his religious enemies.

Much that has been written or said about the Hashashin is probably legend, not fact. People traveling through the Middle East often told wild stories about them. The Italian explorer Marco Polo added colorful details to his stories about the Hashashin.

Some accounts suggest the Hashashin were responsible for hundreds of assassinations over two centuries. Most followers of the Old Man were farmers. They became assassins when the Old Man gave them orders. Then they

A 19th-century engraving of what Shaykh-al-Hashishim might have looked like.

An illustration from 1092 of an assassination by a Hashashin.

would travel throughout the Middle East to do the Old Man's bidding.

It's said the Hashashin approached their targets in public. They wore disguises to get closer. Then they killed their victims with daggers. They weren't afraid of being caught or killed.

Between 1256 and 1258, the Mongols drove the Hashashin out of Iran. Around 1273, a Mamluk sultan named Baybars wiped out the group in Syria.

1050
Estimated year the Old Man of the Mountain was born.

- The Hashashin is one of the most feared secret societies in history.
- Members killed religious enemies by order of their leader, the Old Man of the Mountain.
- Hashashin didn't fear being caught or killed.

THINK ABOUT IT

Throughout history, many wars have started because of religious conflicts. What are some reasons why this might happen?

Molly Maguires: Fighting for Workers' Rights

The Molly Maguires was a secret society with roots in 1840s Ireland. But the group is best known for its activities in the United States during the 1860s and 1870s.

The mid-nineteenth century was a time of mass Irish migration. From 1850 to 1929, more than four million Irish immigrated to the United States. Many took jobs in coal mining. It was hard, dangerous work. Miners worked long hours for little pay. Mines had few safety features. Owners didn't want to pay for them.

Members of the Molly Maguires grew upset with working conditions. They decided to act. They set fires, destroyed equipment, and attacked supervisors. They also threatened mine officials, warning their terror would not stop until conditions improved.

In 1873, the president of the Reading Railroad wanted to destroy

20
Number of suspected Molly Maguires who were executed.

- The Molly Maguires society formed in Ireland in the 1840s.
- Members in the United States fought to improve working conditions in mines.
- A detective gave information about the society to police.

WHAT ABOUT THE NAME?

Some people wonder where the name of this secret Irish society came from. Many believe it references a widow named Molly Maguire in Ireland. It's said she refused to leave her home after a landlord ordered her out. To honor Molly's spirit of resistance, some men in the society even dressed in women's clothing.

the Molly Maguires. He hired the Pinkerton Detective Agency to help. An Irishman named James McParlan pretended to be a coal miner named James McKenna. He spent two years working in the mines among members of the Molly Maguires. He gained their trust, learned their secrets, and turned them in to the police. Many members of the Molly Maguires were tried and executed for their crimes.

James McParland in 1880.

8

P.E.O. Sisterhood: Women Helping Women

Some secret societies can't stay secret, no matter how hard they try. They do such good work they can't stay in the shadows. The P.E.O. Sisterhood is one.

The P.E.O. Sisterhood is a society for women. It helps female students around the world go to college. It does so regardless of a student's age, background, ethnicity, or religion.

The group was founded as a secret women's society in 1869. Seven students at Iowa Wesleyan College in Mount Pleasant, Iowa, started it. The group later expanded to include women who weren't at the college.

The P.E.O. Sisterhood has been helping female students for 150 years. Today it has about 250,000 members. It has awarded more than $300 million globally in grants, loans, and other gifts. The awards help women advance their education.

For many years, the group carried out its mission mostly in secret. Few people knew about it. In 2005, the P.E.O. Sisterhood decided to reveal itself to the world. A public relations campaign called "It's OK to talk about P.E.O." gave the group greater exposure so its members could do more good.

Today the P.E.O. Sisterhood is more widely known, but it still has a few

P.E.O. cofounder Hattie Briggs Bousquet.

Iowa Wesleyan College, where the group was founded in 1869.

secrets. For example, officials have never explained what P.E.O. means. In 2008, the group announced they stood for "Philanthropic Educational Organization." It also admitted the original meaning was different. Only society members know the true meaning.

105,000
Number of women the P.E.O. Sisterhood has helped, as of 2018.

- The P.E.O. Sisterhood was formed in 1869 to help women advance their education.
- Long a secret society, the group went public in 2005.
- The true meaning of the letters P.E.O. is still a secret to nonmembers.

THINK ABOUT IT

Why might girls and women need financial help to advance their learning? What barriers to education do female students face around the world?

9

Golden Dawn Society: Magic and the Occult

In 1880s London, many people believed in the supernatural. William Wynn Westcott was one. In 1887, the Englishman discovered a manuscript written in a cipher. He decoded it. Westcott believed he had found an important document about the occult.

The Hermetic Order of the Golden Dawn, also known as the

1897 portrait of William Wynn Westcott.

3
Number of Orders, or status levels, in Golden Dawn society.

- The society dates to 1887, when many people were interested in the supernatural.
- Members were people who were interested in the occult.
- Fighting among its founders helped lead to the end of the society.

Golden Dawn, was built on Westcott's work. He and two friends started the secret society. They attracted members like the poet W.B. Yeats, who went on to win a Nobel Prize. And Sir Arthur Conan Doyle, author of the Sherlock Holmes stories. Bram Stoker, author of "Dracula," might have been a member. But the Golden Dawn wasn't for men only. Women could join, too. One was Maud Gonne, an Irish revolutionary and actor.

The group studied magic and the supernatural. They learned about astrology and how to read tarot cards. They were interested in paranormal activities. They believed they could call on occult forces with special rituals.

The Golden Dawn was popular for a time, but it didn't last long. Fighting among the founders was one reason why. They disagreed on how to lead the organization. By 1903, the sun had set on the Golden Dawn.

Aleister Crowley in 1916.

REVEALING SECRETS

Aleister Crowley was a Golden Dawn member who became famous after sharing society secrets. He did so in *The Equinox*. This series about the supernatural was published beginning in 1909. Many who held Golden Dawn beliefs didn't like what Crowley had done.

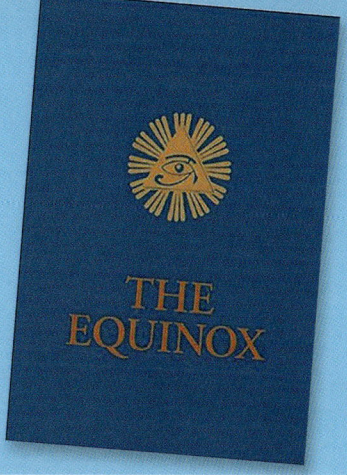

10
IBPOE: Elks for Blacks

Members march in 1963.

In 1868, in New York City, 15 white men founded a secret society. It was called the Benevolent and Protective Order of Elks (BPOE). Known as the Elks, the society began as a social organization. It claimed to stand for charity, justice, brotherly love, and loyalty.

But the Elks didn't show these qualities when B.F. Howard and Arthur J. Riggs tried to join. Both men were black. Because of that, the Elks said no.

Instead of giving up, Howard and Riggs started their own group. They decided it would be better and more

500,000
Number of IBPOE members across 1,500 lodges worldwide as of 2018.

- The Elks society was established by white men in 1868.
- People of color couldn't join, so two black men set up their own Elks lodge.
- By the early 1900s, black men and women were both able to socialize in IBPOE lodges.

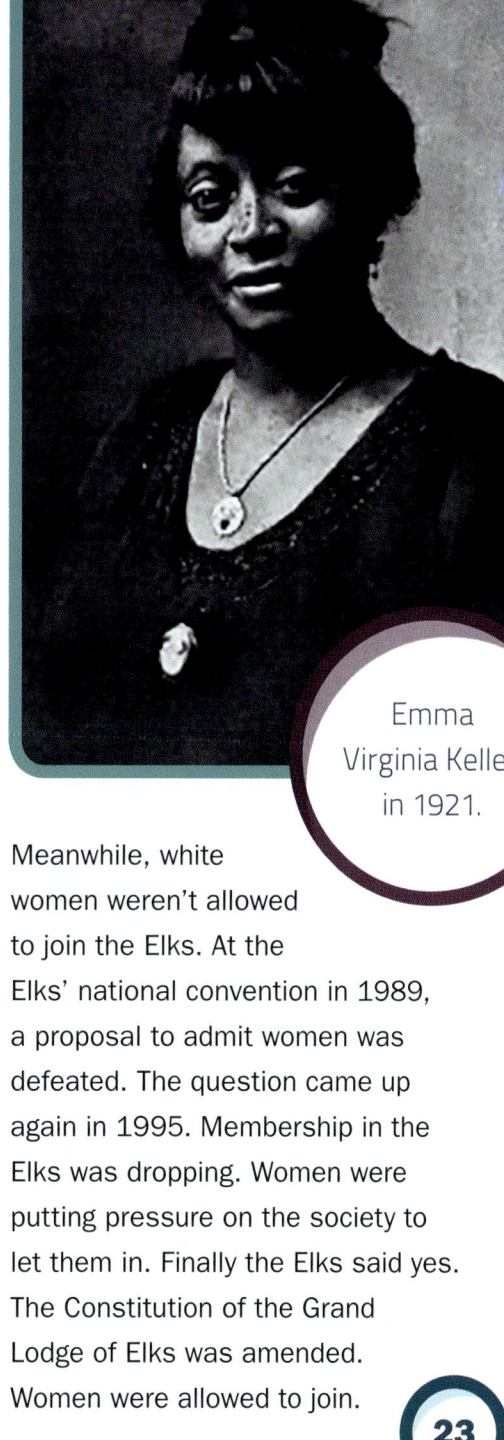

Emma Virginia Kelley in 1921.

equal than the Elks they weren't allowed to join. The Improved Benevolent and Protective Order of Elks (IBPOE) was formed in 1897. The first lodge was in Cincinnati, Ohio.

In the early twentieth century, IBPOE lodges became popular places for black men to spend their free time. In 1902, a black woman named Emma Virginia Kelley started an organization called the Daughters of the Elks in Virginia. It became part of the IBPOE.

Meanwhile, white women weren't allowed to join the Elks. At the Elks' national convention in 1989, a proposal to admit women was defeated. The question came up again in 1995. Membership in the Elks was dropping. Women were putting pressure on the society to let them in. Finally the Elks said yes. The Constitution of the Grand Lodge of Elks was amended. Women were allowed to join.

Bilderberg Group: Global Secrecy

It was 1954, just nine years after the end of World War II. People on both sides of the Atlantic were concerned. They thought the United States and Europe weren't working together as closely as they should. They arranged a meeting between leading citizens.

The meeting took place from May 29–31 at the Hotel De Bilderberg in the Netherlands.

Leaders in politics, economics, business, and culture came for informal discussions. Ever since, the Bilderberg Meetings has been an annual conference. It is the world's most secretive gathering of high-powered global elites.

The meetings are held in fancy hotels in beautiful locations. They are always closed to the public. Different people are invited each year. Journalists aren't allowed.

The Hotel De Bilderberg, where the first meeting took place in 1954.

150
Maximum number of people invited to the Bilderberg Group's conference each year.

- The first Bilderberg Meetings took place in 1954.
- Political, business, and cultural leaders from Europe and North America are invited.
- Cameras aren't allowed into the event, which has led to conspiracy theories about the group.

The secrecy has led to many conspiracy theories. Does the Bilderberg Group want to control the world? Are they trying to influence governments to protect their own power and wealth? Do they want to form a single government? Some members have denied this idea. But others have said that creating one global community could be good for the world.

Armed guards admit only those who are invited.

The group does share the names of the people attending. It also reveals the topics discussed during the conference. Members often say they talk about ways to promote peace and grow economic opportunity. But because cameras aren't allowed in, no one knows if what they say is true.

12
Black Hand Society: The Spark That Started WWI

Dragutin Dimitrijević (center) with members in 1915.

There have been, and still are, many secret groups all over the world. Some do good and others don't. But only one has been responsible for starting a world war.

In 1911, a Serbian army officer named Dragutin Dimitrijević helped start a secret group called Union or Death. It became known as the Black Hand. At the time, some Serbs outside Serbia were living under Habsburg (Austrian) or Ottoman (Turkish) rule. The Black Hand wanted all Serbs to live in one nation. They used terrorism to further their cause.

The Black Hand was behind the assassination of the Austrian archduke Franz Ferdinand and his wife, Sophia. On June 28, 1914, they were riding through Sarajevo in an open car. An 18-year-old student named Gavrilo Princip shot them both. Protests and riots followed. On July 28, Austria-Hungary declared war on Serbia. After that, because of alliances between various countries, a world war was unstoppable.

SPREADING THE WORD

The Black Hand did not rely on violence alone to accomplish its goals. The society also used propaganda. Black Hand members spread lies to influence what people believed about the government. People who believed these lies often joined the group. This helped the Black Hand become even more powerful.

200
Approximate number of Black Hand members imprisoned in 1917.

- The Black Hand was formed to unify Serbians.
- The society assassinated archduke Franz Ferdinand, triggering World War I.
- Black Hand members were imprisoned or executed in 1917.

For a few years after the assassination, the Black Hand was an influential force in Serbia. But government officials worried they might try to take over the country. In 1917, hundreds of Black Hand members were arrested on treason charge. They were sent to prison. The leaders were executed. The Black Hand was no more. But the Great War would continue for another year. More than 16 million people died.

A members meeting in 1910.

Fact Sheet

- In 1918, descendants of Geronimo, the famous Apache leader, accused Skull and Bones of stealing their ancestor's remains. In 2009, members of the Apache tribe filed a lawsuit against the secret society. The case was dismissed.

- One thing the Freemasons require of all members is a belief in a higher power. At the same time, officials insist the society is not a religious organization. When Freemasons gather, they don't discuss religion.

- The Odd Fellows help people who are researching their family history. Those with ancestors who were members of the group can contact the lodge for information about a relative's time and activity in the society.

- Many people think that Illuminati founder Adam Weishaupt was against religion. When asked about this, he said it wasn't true. He did say that he often disagreed with ways religion was practiced and imposed on people.

- Some members of the Molly Maguires found guilty of murder insisted they were innocent. That didn't stop officials from hanging them. Many historians today believe some society members were falsely accused.

- The P.E.O. Sisterhood operates Cottey College in Nevada, Missouri. This is a liberal arts and science college for women. Students may choose to pursue a two-year or four-year degree at the private school.

Glossary

assassination
The killing of a person for political or religious reasons.

charity
The giving of money or objects for the purpose of helping others.

cipher
A secret code in which one letter or word stands for another.

controversial
Something that causes people to argue or disagree.

Crusades
Religious wars that took place between Christians and Muslims in the Middle Ages, the time in European history from about 500–1500 CE.

dissolve
To close down or put an end to.

elite
Having extraordinary power or wealth.

Medieval
Having to do with the Middle Ages, the time in European history from about 500–1500 CE.

occult
Having to do with supernatural powers or magic.

philanthropic
Done for the purpose of helping others.

Pilgrim
A person who travels to a holy place.

politics
Activities and issues associated with government.

propaganda
False or misleading information meant to support a point of view.

sect
A religious group that is part of a larger group. The members of a sect have similar beliefs. Their beliefs may not be the same as the main group.

treason
Crimes against one's own government.

For More Information

Books

Forest, Christopher. *Secret American People: From Secret Societies to Secret Agents.* Minneapolis, MN: Capstone Press, 2009.

Roxburgh, Ellis. *Conspiracies: Who's Hiding What?* New York: Lucent Books, 2018.

Walker, Kathryn. *Mysteries of the Mind.* New York: Crabtree Publishing, 2009

Visit 12StoryLibrary.com

Scan the code or use your school's login at **12StoryLibrary.com** for recent updates about this topic and a full digital version of this book. Enjoy free access to:

- Digital ebook
- Breaking news updates
- Live content feeds
- Videos, interactive maps, and graphics
- Additional web resources

Note to educators: Visit 12StoryLibrary.com/register to sign up for free premium website access. Enjoy live content plus a full digital version of every 12-Story Library book you own for every student at your school.

Index

assassination, 4, 14-15, 26-27, 30

Bilderberg Group, 24-25
Bousquet, Hattie Briggs, 18

charity, 8-9, 11, 22, 30
Christian, 6-7, 30

de Payens, Hugues, 6
Dimitrijević, Dragutin, 26

education, 18-19

Franz Ferdinand, 26-27
fraternity, 12
Freemasons, 8-9, 28

Golden Dawn Society, 20-21
Government, 6, 8, 25, 27, 30

Hashashin, 14-15

Improved Benevolent and Protective Order of Elks (IBPOE), 22-23

Kelly, Emma Virginia, 23
Knights Templar, 6-7

Molly Maguires, 16-17

occult, 20-21, 30
Odd Fellows, 10-11, 28

Old Man of the Mountain, 14-15

P.E.O. Sisterhood, 18-19, 29
philanthropic, 19, 30

Rebekah's, 11

Skull and Bones, 4-5, 28

The Black Hand, 26-27

war, 15, 24, 26-27, 30

Yale, 4-5

About the Author
Tammy Gagne has written more than 200 books for adults and children. She resides in northern New England with her husband and son. One of her favorite pastimes is visiting schools to talk to kids about the writing process.

READ MORE FROM 12-STORY LIBRARY

Every 12-Story Library Book is available in many fomats. For more information, visit 12StoryLibrary.com

WITHDRAWN

Albert Carlton-Cashiers
Community Library
PO Box 2127
Cashiers NC 28717